Empty World
Meditations & Practices For Immediate Peace of Mind

Table Of Contents

Slow down.
Become aware of your breathing.
Nothing more than that for now.
Just notice the sensations of the breath rising and falling.
Do not force the breath in nor out.
Just breathe.
Be aware of your breathing.

Notice the breath rises and falls.
The sounds around you rise and fall.
Thoughts and feelings come and go.
Remain in being the awareness of what comes and goes.
Not the participant.

Everything you perceive will come and go.
Notice your perception does not come and go.

You are now meditating.

Introduction

This book contains a collection of powerful practices and meditations for finding immediate serenity. You need no experience in meditation or any background in spirituality. If you already have a background in meditation and spirituality the practices in this book will deepen what you have discovered already. These practices and meditations are simple and direct using plain language. All that is required to find peace immediately is the sincerity of the student.

It does not matter if you have busy thoughts or you find it difficult to focus for long periods of time, the practices in this book have been developed with modern problems in mind. Taking small amounts of time away from external distractions is powerful even if you keep feeling agitated. In time the patience will effortlessly grow within you. Even finding one second of inner stillness is enough of a seed to allow true serenity to take root. Practicing everything within this book will allow peace to flourish. Regardless of the nature of your psychological pain the practices in this book will alleviate your suffering.

Many people who have suffered from problems such as overthinking, anxiety, depression and stress have found relief and recovered fully through contemplative practices such as meditation.

If you begin to feel frustrated that you are not 'Getting it' do not worry this is very common. Slow down. There is no rush at all. Questions and sticking points may arise but through the practices outlined in this book they will dissolve and intuition will take their place. Patience is a skill that can be trained. Simply return to the practices and meditations in this book with confidence, approach with a natural curiosity and a sincere wish to find a sense of inner peace.

If you want to practice Empty World as a Course, in sequential order practice each of the five sections (both the informal and the formal practices) contained within every day for seven days before moving on to the next section.

Alternatively, you may find a particular meditation or practice truly resonates with you. If this is the case there will be a very good reason for it, a certain specific principle contained here may speak to an old or stubborn pain within you, perhaps the primary cause of your suffering. If this is the case simply devote time and attention to that particular practice until inner peace is found. The light of your conscious awareness will burn away all of these shadows.

The first two sections of this book utilise similar practices you may have encountered before. The final three sections are unique practices developed specifically for this book. These are the Empty World principles.

Before beginning any meditation or practice within this book it's important to recognise the intention here is to seek peace of mind. The intention of meditation is not to seek happiness nor try to attain something new, but instead to uncover the peace and joy that is present naturally within you. You naturally reside within a state of peace and stillness, it must simply be discovered.

Each section in this book contains a practice with an underlying principle that can be utilised in daily life and contemplated at your own pace. Each section also contains a formal meditation with an allotted time that develops the principle of the section.

To practice the formal meditations read each line slowly and carefully, then take as many breaths needed to truly assimilate the pointing. When it feels natural to do so move on to the next line.

Throughout this book, where you see the — symbol take some time to rest and reflect.

—

Terminology
'Meditation' here refers to formal, structured practice with allotted time.
'Meditative Practice' is informal and can be practiced anywhere for any length of time.

1. Stay Present

A. Staying Present In Daily Life (Meditative Practice)

Have you ever noticed that it's only ever the present? There is no future, what we call the future never arrives. There is no past, what we call the past has been and gone. Isn't it odd that we spend so much of our time and energy worrying about something that simply doesn't exist? Become aware of the present moment as it is right now. Notice how much calmer the reality around you truly is than your thoughts would have you believe. Is anything really happening right now, other than in your mind?

When you find yourself lost in an uncomfortable state of mind bring your attention fully into the present moment. This is a core principle of finding peace that is mentioned in every spirituality, religion, philosophy, discipline and science dedicated to resolving psychological suffering. This need not be complicated, just find presence through recognising the reality of the present moment. Experience Now directly without analysing, interpreting or creating an opinion, simply notice and observe what is.

Although this is simple you might recognise this is not easy. Your mind is always attempting to pull your thoughts towards the future or to the past. This is okay, predicting the future and analyzing the past is what the mind does naturally, but taking some time to refocus into the reality of life is an enormous relief. The reality of life is that it's always the present moment, everything else is just a thought.

Wherever you are you can bring your awareness into the present moment. There is no need for a special position and you do not have to close your eyes. You could be anywhere at any time. In the que at a supermarket, walking through a busy place, or even at work. It is common for people to devote a huge amount of energy into negative thoughts when stressed and busy, often unable to focus on a single thought but enduring a racing mind lost in a frantic stream of thoughts and feelings, it does not have to be this way.

By staying fully present, you step out of the stream of thoughts and stand safely on the side watching the thoughts go by. Like standing on a railway platform and not getting onto any train that stops, don't be tempted to get on board, just let the doors close and off it goes.

Do not worry, when staying present you will remain conscious and aware of everything that is going on. In fact, you will be able to do so with far more clarity and precision as you won't be lost in daydreaming but instead perceiving the world exactly as it is.

When you have become aware you are lost in thoughts and recognising your thoughts are making you upset, angry, frustrated or low try this practice. Do not worry if the changes in perception are subtle at first, once the process has started it will naturally become automatic and your conscious attention on the present moment will deepen.

Simply become aware of breathing, this is always available to you.
Just notice the sensations of breathing.
No need to force the breath in or practice any special technique.
Notice all of the feelings arising within you but for now don't get involved in them.
Place no judgment or opinion on them.
Simply observing what is.

Notice all of the sounds around you but not attempting to label or place an opinion on them.
Notice what is already here, what is actually here.
Simply what is.

Allow no energy to go towards that which isn't happening in the here and now.
Just observe what is.

There is no future.
You are not ignoring the future, but recognising that it simply doesn't exist.
Even planning, apprehension and prediction are only thoughts arising within the present.
Anything important will be taken care of, you've done enough worrying for now just leave it all alone.

There is no past.
You are not neglecting the past, but simply recognising that it doesn't exist.
Even regret, guilt, injustice and bad memories are all thoughts and images arising in the present.
Anything important will be processed by your mind of it's own accord within the present, simply be aware of anything arising but do not get involved.

—

Be free to practice this anywhere at any time.
This could even be as you travel from one place to another, perhaps from home to work.

In particular, see if it's possible to do this at the first sign you feel negative emotions arising in you.

Many have found inner peace through this practice alone.

B. Presence (Meditation - 10 Minutes)

To practice this formal meditation find a space in which you most likely won't be disturbed for 10 minutes or so. Read each line slowly and carefully, then take as many breaths needed to truly assimilate the pointing. When it feels natural to do so move on to the next line.

Begin by simply becoming aware of the breath.
Notice the sensations of the breath as it rises and falls.
There is no need to force the breath in nor out.
Simply observe the sensations of breathing.
Notice the breath will naturally deepen itself.
There is no pressure to do this, just observe.
If some restlessness or agitation arises simply observe this too.
You have this time now to just be still.
Take one minute or so to truly connect with the breath.

—

Open awareness to all of the sounds around you.
These may be very subtle, just be open to them.
Do not attempt to label or place an opinion upon the sounds.
Just observe them as they are.
Continuing to observe the breath also.
Nothing will disturb your meditation now.
Take a minute or so to observe the sounds around you.

—

If you find that your mind has wandered to thoughts of future or past,
There is no need to be frustrated, this is simply the mind doing what it does naturally.
When you become aware this has happened, simply reconnect with the breath and the sounds around you.
Perfectly safe and confident now within this present moment.
Nothing to be done.
Just being.

Take one minute or so to recognise even thoughts of future or past arise within the present moment yet the present moment never changes.

—

Notice the character of the thoughts your mind wanders to.
Thoughts try to pull you forwards into planning, or prediction about something that may or may not happen.
Memories arise of past events resurfacing are trying to claim your attention.
There is nothing wrong with the mind doing this.
Anything important can be dealt with when it's appropriate but not right now, leave it alone.
Regardless of the nature of the thoughts or feelings, simply apply awareness only.
No analysis required.

Do not get involved with any thought or feeling at all
Simply observe the thought rising and then falling away.
Stay fully here, fully now.

Notice that right now, in this present moment.
Nothing is actually happening other than in your mind.
Apply the courage to simply remain here and now.
Take a minute or so to practice this now.

—

2. Let Go

A. Drop The Story (Meditative Practice)

Who are you without your story?
If you were to close the book of The Story Of You for a few minutes do any problems remain?

There are many valid painful experiences from the past that cause us pain in the present. Similarly, there are many worthwhile concerns about the future that cause us pain in the present. How the past and future relates to us in the present is created by the meaning we attach to certain events or predictions. This meaning we attach to our life situation can be thought of as a story. It may be a useful story, it may be a story we have been telling ourselves for a long time, but it remains a story nonetheless.

Imagine if you could close that story for a while.

Naturally we are very reluctant to consider ceasing that story as we have come to believe it is who we are and worried about what will happen to us without it. We may also have some very significant events in our lives that we wish to hold on to. But it is precisely this willingness to let go that makes this practice so powerful.

Have you ever wondered where these massive, significant life events go when you are asleep?
Similarly ask yourself if your problems still cause you anxiety and stress while you are asleep at night?
Where do they go exactly?

We might say they are temporarily suspended but they are still 'there'
But they only re-appear once we begin thinking about them again.
If we did not think about them again they would vanish.

What if we could take a moment to simply drop it all?
For a moment not trying to fix the past nor improve the future, not attaching any meaning at all to the present. The entire story both of what has happened to you and what you have done. This is all a story that only exists in your mind in the present moment.

So what would happen if you simply stopped telling the story for a moment?
Simply drop it *all*.

No complicated practice or arduous discipline needed just close the book on The Story Of You.
Many people find full enlightenment spontaneously and instantly by doing just that.
Close the book.

We can get it back later if we wish, but just for a moment close the entire book and just leave it.
What remains of your problems and pain without your story?
Within the here and now, experiencing life as it truly is.
No story at all, just awareness of the present moment.

Naturally there are some problems that seem to persist.
But see which ones don't.

Just drop them, perfectly safe to do this now.

—

When engaged in daily life and you begin to feel stress and tension building up try bringing your attention into the present moment and see if there is actually any immediate cause of the stress and tension.

There may be some very real stressors occurring, but these become amplified by certain unhelpful thought patterns which relate to our personal story. In this way you might find you attach meaning to unrelated problems, increasing the pain from the negative state of mind.

"This always happens to me."
"The world needs to stop being like this."
"People always treat me this way."
"I need to get better at…"
"This is typical."
"I'm always like this."

When you notice these patterns arising and causing you to be miserable practice the powerful technique of simply not engaging with the thoughts at all.
Do not try to argue with your thoughts,
Do not try to bury or destroy your thoughts.
Simply acknowledge they are there and do not get involved at all.

Within the present moment, there is no story.

Ask yourself "Is the pain I am experiencing necessary?"
If it isn't, then it's likely you have attached your story to the circumstances.
Stop the story and simply feel whatever is happening.
Anything that happens within the present can be dealt with.

At first this will be easier to do when you are alone but with practice (sometimes immediately) it becomes possible to fully drop the entire story the moment you realise it has begun.

Naturally we feel we cannot escape these as we have come to believe this story is our entire life.
But there was a time before the story began wasn't there?
See what happens when the book is closed.
Have you gone anywhere?

Your breath continues, the sun still rises and falls.
The moon comes out at night.
The birds sing, the planet turns.
Life goes on, yours included.
Your body continues it's processes.

The world around you and within you carries on.

Simply stay out of the whole thing for a while.

Now as yourself, if it's possible to step out and close the book
Is The Story Of You really you?
—

B. The Balloon (Meditation - 15 Mins)
To practice this formal meditation find a space in which you most likely won't be
disturbed for 15 minutes or so. Read each line slowly and carefully, then take as many
breaths needed to truly assimilate the pointing. When it feels natural to do so move on
to the next line.

Turning off all devices and screens.
If there is some noise or distraction during this time it is okay, nothing has to pull your
attention away from the meditation.
Finding any position that feels most comfortable and appropriate for you.
If you choose to take a position laying down, try not to fall asleep.
Give this meditation as much focus and sincerity as you can.
Slow down, there is no rush.

Begin by becoming aware of the breath as it rises and falls.

Notice the sensations of breathing, but applying no analysis.
There is no 'good' breathing or 'bad' breathing. There is simply breathing.
There is nothing to be done now, no pressure or anything to worry about.
Simply breathe, allowing the breath to naturally deepen itself.
Take a minute or two to simply be aware of the breath now.

—

Notice as you do this that thoughts naturally arise and fall.
All of the stories and situations that have been playing on your mind may arise during
this meditation, pay them no attention at all.
Just be aware that thoughts and feelings are there.
Simply allow them to rise and fall just as the breath rises and falls.
Do not follow thoughts anywhere, they are not needed now.

—

Now, visualise that you are holding a helium balloon.
The upwards pull is incredibly powerful, trying to escape your hold.

To this balloon, we are going to attach some things that we aren't going to need for this
meditation.

Firstly your name: Your first name, last name, nicknames or titles you may have.
Attached to the balloon.

Now any and all numbers that you feel may represent you in some way: Age, height,
weight, salary and phone number.
All attached to the balloon.

Now, any personal history or thoughts of future.
You can get anything back later that you wish to take back.
For the purposes of this meditation, *all* personal history and *all* thoughts of future,
including ambitions, dreams and even positive memories. Just for the duration of this
meditation.
All attached to the balloon.

Lastly, any judgments about self. Positive or negative.
Any sense of self-image.
Who you are as a person, if you're a good person or bad person, how you look and act,
thoughts and feelings about your current life situation.
Quite easy now to simply attach to the balloon.

Now, with these things attached, this balloon has a powerful upwards pull, trying hard to
escape from your hold.

Let go.

Take a minute or two here as the balloon safely sails away.

—

Notice that without everything we had attached, the breath continues.
The body's processes continue.
Simply remain open and empty now.
Fully spacious.
Everything that arises now simply drifts by.
Hold on to nothing at all.

Continue to breathe deeply

—

You may wish to spend longer in this meditation once serenity is found.
When you feel ready to begin moving again.
As you go about your life you will find the things that you had let go of during the meditation.

Don't be so quick to pick everything back up again, you don't have to carry anything with you.

—

3. **Empty Room**

A. Emptying (Meditative Practice)

The way we perceive ourselves in relation to others is the source of unnecessary stress, worry, anger and frustration.

In the previous section we considered the powerful question of where your problems go when you sleep, they appear to temporarily vanish.
Perhaps an even better question is where do 'You' go when you sleep?

Consider the fact that every problem 'You' have relates to 'You' by definition, otherwise they would not be your problems.

—

Even if the problem you have is in relation to something outside of yourself, it is still your feelings towards the problem that is the essence of the suffering the problem is creating. If the problem can be fixed then it's not a problem, if the problem can't be fixed then it's also not a problem as there isn't anything you can do about it.

Many of the issues you face simply do not exist at all other than in your mind. There are other issues that cause unavoidable pain and this may require wise and intuitive guidance. But with any issue that arises begin from the position of asking if you can simply avoid it altogether. If the issue cannot be avoided lessen it's emotional drain by not attaching anything unnecessary to the issue.

Consider that the suffering created by the issue cannot exist if you were to temporarily suspend the concept of 'You'. Pain may persist, discomfort may persist, there may be action required to alter something in the external or internal world, however if you were to remain fully within the present moment as awareness only without any concept of individual identity, the suffering vanishes.

"I am in pain." is replaced by "There is pain." which may seem like a subtle difference at first, but soon becomes liberating.

How to achieve this state?
Begin by asking:
Who are 'You' exactly?

As a short exercise here try to explain who you are without referencing the future or the past, only what is in this moment.

—

Recognise also that your body and mind carry on their natural functions without your involvement.

—

We spend a great deal of time trying to fix our self-image, trying to improve ourselves or increase our self-worth. You may not have previously considered the option to simply leave the whole thing and remain fully empty of any concept of identity or self for a while, just as it is when you sleep, but instead you are fully awake.

Do not worry, you can get 'You' back at any moment if you choose to.

When you find you are experiencing negative mind states in relation to your sense of self such as feeling low self-esteem, worried about how you are being perceived, embarrassing memories, being treated unfairly or any anxiety about oneself as a person try the following practice.

Wherever you find yourself simply take note of and observe everything around you. Connect with the breath and bring yourself fully into the here and now by simply ignoring any ideas, thoughts or feelings about past or future. Ask yourself if there are any problems happening right now in this moment other than in your mind?

Take a moment or two to simply rest within the present moment and already the peace will begin to flourish within you.

Placing no opinion or label on anything around you.
Now with a strong visual image in mind of the colors and sounds around you.
Take note in vivid detail the space around you.
Sounds, temperature, colours and light.

If it's possible and safe to do so close your eyes for moments during this practice.
Do not worry, no one will notice.

Breathing deeply and connecting with the breath now
Visualise the space you are in to be fully empty of all people including yourself.

There is no need to invent a reason for how or why, there is simply nobody here.
Be as though the space is empty.
There is simply nobody here.
There never was and there never will be.

Really do this now.
Your mind will try to invent reasons why the room is empty but pay no attention to this
Simply become the pure light of consciousness by fully emptying the room.

Notice that your body continues it's natural functions without your involvement.
Notice the world doesn't stop when you stop analysing the world.

Your consciousness here can now function unblocked by the mind created projection of self-image.

Free to enjoy the present moment without spending energy upholding a self-image.

—

B. Empty Room (Meditation - 20 Minutes)

To practice this formal meditation find a space in which you most likely won't be disturbed for 20 minutes or so. Read each line slowly and carefully, then take as many breaths needed to truly assimilate the pointing. When it feels natural to do so move on to the next line.

Once you have begun no noise or disturbance will pull your attention away from this meditation.

Take a moment to find a position that feels most appropriate for you but be aware we will be staying awake during this meditation.

Begin by becoming aware of the breath.
Observe the sensations of breathing as the breath rises and falls.
Place no analysis or opinion upon the sensations of breathing.
Simply allow and observe.
If there are thoughts and feelings arising pay no attention to these.
Instead choosing to focus on the breath and allowing thought to come and go.
Take a minute or so to do this now.
Take as much time as needed to really do this today.
There is no hurry.

—

Look around the room.
Take note of the character of the light upon the objects in the room.
Observe the colours and details.
Notice the stillness and the calmness of the physical world.
But placing no name or label upon any object.
See if it's possible to simply take in all of the visual images automatically.
Without spending any effort on analysing or interpreting what you see.
Just observe what is.
Take a minute or two to do this now.
There is no rush or hurry.

—

When you are ready, you are going to close your eyes.
With eyes closed fully open your awareness to the sensations of breathing.
The sensations in the body.

Stay fully present in the here and now.
But placing no analysis or interpretation upon anything at all.

Take a minute or so to do this now.
Once you find a little more stillness reopen your eyes.

—

Continuing to breathe deeply and really let go now.
Letting go of all stories, names and labels.
Letting go of all history and future.
Letting go of all people just for this time.
Just fully immersed in what is Now.
Fully safe and secure in this present moment.
The only moment there ever is or will be.

In a moment, you will close your eyes and visualize the room as though you were not in it.
As though the room is empty of all people.
Do not spend any attention on trying to figure out how or why this is
Just a simple visualization of the room with nobody in it.

Take a moment to do this now.

—

Relax into this.
No need for how or why.
Just being fully empty in the here and now.
Nobody here.

—

Notice that your body continues to process it's functions
The breath continues.
Even thoughts and feelings still come and go.
But now observed from a far calmer space of emptiness.

—

4. Empty Spaces

A. Empty Self (Meditative Practice)

Consider how much your suffering is caused by other people.

—

Directly through their immediate influence on you and indirectly as a result of your interactions with them. On an individual scale and with the world as a whole much of your suffering is caused by your relationship with other people.

Through immediate influence people can upset you and directly cause stress and misery. The list of how someone's actions upon you can cause you suffering is almost endless. Wouldn't it be incredible to learn that most and sometimes all of this suffering can be effortlessly avoided, giving you the space and freedom to truly enjoy your life?

A powerful practice for finding peace is to spend time alone. Not only to spend time alone but also while alone to cease obsessively thinking about other people. To be fully present in the here and now and simply enjoy life as it is, without stressful thoughts of your effect upon others or their effects upon you. Spending time doing this heals the body and mind as a return to your natural self is achieved.

Recognise that other people can have no effect upon your pure consciousness in the present moment. They can only have an effect on your mind created self-image. Recognising this subtle difference is very powerful and many people find inner peace just from recognising this alone. By bringing your attention fully into the present moment in pure observation you completely remove other people's power to have a negative effect upon your state of mind as there will be no self-image to have an effect upon.

Now here is the most powerful practice of all, recognise that when we are obsessing over other people, singularly, as a group, or as a whole we are actually obsessing over our mind created image of that person or people. Ultimately this is just a thought and therefore an illusion.

We cannot alter other people's self-image and we have very little control over our own. Your own self-image requires you to imagine how another is perceiving you and this task is impossible. You can choose to recognise this mind created self-image as false and thereby remove yourself entirely from the source of pain forever.

By doing this you will regain control over your own emotional state once and for all.

—

As an informal practice. Find some time where you can be fully alone. Getting into natural surroundings for this is preferable. Turn off all screens and devices. Notice the calmness and stillness of the world around you when there is nobody around. There is a natural joy in the world even when nothing is happening.

Notice your emotional reactions to the prospect of spending time alone. Often people are avoidant of being alone with their own thoughts for fear of what might arise. But there is nothing to fear. Thoughts are just thoughts and they will rise and fall in their own time. There is great freedom in the ability to be alone and comfortable with just yourself.

Now in this space when you are alone with no screens or devices on, there is nobody around to perceive you. There is nobody around to call you by your name, to remind you of who you are supposed to be or to reaffirm your personality. Where has your personality gone if you are fully silent and alone?

Your personality can only exist when there are other people around to perceive you. If you are alone within the present moment the personality vanishes.

If this personality which you have come to believe is you can simply vanish, can it really be you?

—

Understand that when thoughts and feelings rise and fall, when observed consciously, they are processed in a very healthy way that will lead to great insight and wisdom. When alone we are free from others approving or disproving of us and so our natural intuition can flourish. Ordinarily our creative intuitions and insights are subject to the opinions of others which is occasionally useful but most of the time is not.

Begin trusting yourself as you are the only one who can possibly know what is best for you. If you trust yourself your life will become smooth and energised.

Often the best courses of action in life become apparent only when you have had time away from distractions and outside influence and instead let your natural intuition guide you.

This can be uncomfortable to begin with if you are not accustomed to being alone. But using the following practices will allow the peace and freedom within you to flourish.

Firstly let us understand our self-image so that we might remove the suffering associated with it, then come to a place of acceptance in our relationship to others and with ourselves.

We are constantly trying to alter our self-image to become acceptable to others around us and acceptable to ourselves. Working incredibly hard to be valuable to the group in which we operate, both at work and as part of the world as a whole. This creates a great deal of frustration, anxiety and depression as we are attempting to do something that can't be achieved.

Consider the fact that the image you hold of yourself in your mind cannot possibly be the same as anyone else's image they hold of you. They don't have the same information you have nor the same experience. In addition to that they will always perceive you through the lens of their own perception, which will be coloured entirely by their own personal history and their own self-image.

Now recognise that to someone else you are the very person they are trying to convey their own self-image to. Your perception of them will be absolutely nothing like what they are trying to convey nor will it be in any way similar to what they have in their own mind. In essence we have two illusions attempting to interact.

How much time and energy do you waste trying to control other people's perception of you when by definition this can never be correct?

So with that understanding we come to realize both our own self-image and other people's image of us has to be incorrect. If that is the case then what is the purpose of this self-image in the first place? Even if we believe the self-image is a useful and necessary illusion, the fact remains that it is an illusion.

In modern life self-image and everything attached to it has become a priority but this is a mistake. It is a very fragile state of mind to be in to believe that you actually are the image you have created in your mind.

When your image is attacked or invalidated, you waste enormous amounts of energy trying to defend, protect or alter your image so as not to feel the pain. Again this is a mistake, instead recognising that nothing is actually happening at all is the true defense against this suffering.

B. Empty Spaces (Meditation - 20 Minutes)

To practice this formal meditation find a space in which you most likely won't be disturbed for 20 minutes or so. Read each line slowly and carefully, then take as many breaths needed to truly assimilate the pointing. When it feels natural to do so move on to the next line.

Slow down.
Breathe and become aware of your breathing, nothing more than this.
Rest in total acceptance of what truly is within the here and now.
But placing no analysis or interpretation on anything at all.
Tell yourself no story about this present moment.
Just observing what is.

Whatever state your mind is currently in simply accept and allow.
Observing all thoughts and feelings coming and going.
But placing no analysis or interpretation on any thoughts and feelings.
Just observing what is.

—

Recognising that there is no future and there is no past.
Free yourself from these illusions.
If thoughts of future or past arise simply leave them alone.
Stay in the here and now.
If any restlessness or agitation arises simply observe this also, it will pass.

—

Visualise the space you are in as totally empty.
There is nobody here, not even you.
No need for how or why, just this empty space.

—

Visualise a place that you frequently visit, perhaps a supermarket or park
Imagine the space in vivid detail.
Now visualise that space as fully empty, with nobody there, even during a time it is usually busy.
You are not there either.

This place is fully empty, nobody there now, there never has been and there never will be.
If this proves difficult, focus on particular smaller spaces within the space to begin with.
No need for how or why, simply rest in this image for this time.

—

Visualise your place of work,
Imagine in vivid detail every room, colour and sound.
Now visualise this space as fully empty, with nobody there, even during normal working hours.
You are not there either.
The place is fully empty, nobody there now, there never has been and there never will be.
If this proves difficult, focus on particular smaller spaces within the space to begin with.
No need for how or why, simply rest in this image for this time.

—

When you feel your mind wandering simply return your attention to the breath and the body.
Continue to visualise the space in vivid detail.
Visualise each object, the space, the lighting in the environment, only there are no people anywhere.
No need for how or why.
Just this for now.

—

5. Empty World

A. Conscious Living (Meditative Practice)

When you have spent some time in meditation and practicing emptiness the question arises of how to continue to interact with people who are not fully present and are caught up in their own thoughts, stories and self-image. These are natural and compassionate questions.

Begin by understanding that everyone has a temporary and ever-changing nature. They constantly alter and flow. Who they are today is not who they will be tomorrow. Even those who you are very close to are always changing. Because of this constant fluctuation within the present moment it is a powerful practice to allow others to change and flow without trying to alter or hold on to them. Fully accept and allow someone exactly as they are in the moment and you will feel a far deeper sense of appreciation, belonging, love and kinship. You will begin to gain a deeper insight into people when you see them as an ever changing process rather than a static object.

As a practice, when engaged in a conversation with another person see if it's possible to begin bringing yourself into a more present state of mind while still talking and interacting.

Throughout these practices we have observed it's possible to let go of our own personal story, our past and our future, our self-image and all of the suffering that comes with it. When interacting with others begin from a place of understanding that they are most likely caught entirely within their personal story, past, future and self-image while they interact with you. Also understand this could quite easily be dropped immediately. In this way you begin to see people as they actually are. When you see this you no longer fear people, you no longer need their approval, you no longer worry what they think nor do you try to come across a certain way to them, you can simply enjoy people's company exactly as they are in the present moment and nothing more is required. You are free from people.

Habitually we quickly get pulled into another person's story and begin interacting with their mind projected self-image, instead, see if it's possible to cease analysing every word and sentence they say and instead become conscious of the emotional energy that the person is displaying. The content of the words will still be received and interpreted by your brain only now you are far more conscious of the energy and therefore the true message of what they are trying to communicate.

It is common for people to be saying one thing but meaning another. You will be far more aware of this happening once you have mastered emptiness. You will be able to understand people in far deeper clarity. From a deeper space of presence and consciousness you will be able to respond calmly and confidently if you choose to respond at all. Often simply listening consciously is enough to allow someone to find peace and prevents you from being drawn into unnecessary and exhausting chatter.

By staying empty and conscious you will also no longer have to spend energy trying to analyse conversations and interactions that have happened in the past, nor trying to predict and plan conversations that will happen in the future. Instead you will feel the most healthy words and responses arising within you naturally.

Getting drawn into other people's story affirms their self-image and does not help them. By remaining empty of your own self-image in conversation you no longer amplify the other person's suffering but instead provide space in which they can relax and find peace. By doing so you will continue alleviating and healing your own pain also as you begin to realise truly that you no longer need to spend any energy upholding a false self-image or continue re-affirming your own personal story.

Your natural self is always valuable, worthy and loved by others. Your consciousness becomes the space that suffering cannot reside within.

—

You may also ask the question of how to spend your life if you were to no longer place so much importance on future, without so much emphasis on ambition, goals and desires, no longer placing so much importance on being approved by people or striving to achieve. You might also question morality and question if this practice is in some way selfish or irresponsible. These are compassionate questions.

The truth is that you are free to spend your life however you wish. Your life happens now, not in the future nor in the past. It is happening before your eyes this very moment, the problems in life occur not when we did not worry enough, but when we worried too much. The worry about life becomes more stressful than life itself. Many of our goals when looked at consciously transpire to be nothing more than conditioning, our natural inclination in life produces very different goals. These goals and aspirations are more natural and therefore can be attained sooner. Striving and stressing to achieve goals that we don't actually care to achieve is exhausting and very common.

Problems in life cannot arise from being *too* present.

In conscious, empty presence you find that you no longer wish to continue with negative habits and actions. Being empty and spacious allows your true self to thrive and in doing so you bring your natural gifts, passion and talents to the world. By becoming present you will become healthier and happier, which in turn lightens the world around you and allows others to do the same. Someone who is fully at peace with themselves is incapable of evil, if everyone on earth was at peace, evil and suffering would vanish.

Natural inspiration, inclination and intuition will now be able to flow more freely when you remain conscious, present and empty and you will find that your happiness, satisfaction and peace are not something to be attained, but your natural state of being that has been right here and now your entire life.

B. Empty World (Meditation - 30 Minutes)
To practice this formal meditation find a space in which you most likely won't be disturbed for 30 minutes or so. Read each line slowly and carefully, then take as many breaths needed to truly assimilate the pointing. When it feels natural to do so move on to the next line.

Slow down.
Become aware of your breathing.
Become silent.

—

Notice the sensations in the body, but placing no image or interpretation upon any sensation.
Open your awareness to the sounds around you, but place no name or label upon any sound.
Observe the light and colour in the space around you, but place no label or interpretation upon anything you can see.
Observe any thought and feeling that arises now as no different from any sound or image in the space around you, these are all a part of the same whole.

—

Visualise the world with nobody in it.

—

Everything remains exactly as it is, but just for this time now, there is nobody here.
There is no need for how or why.
There is no need for implication.

Nobody in any cities or towns.
Nobody in any buildings or in any streets.
Nobody around to talk or act.
Nobody in fields or forests.
Nobody in jungles or deserts.
Nobody in mountains or glaciers.
Nobody above and nobody below.
Nobody to the left and nobody to the right.
Nobody inside and nobody outside.

SImply no one anywhere.
There are no implications of this, just that there is no one.

Nature carries on, the sun continues to sail across the sky.
There is light and energy everywhere.
Only now, there is nobody around to witness it.
No more problems now.
No need for interpreting this at all, just for this time.
Allow this visualisation to bring you to a space of peace.

—

There was nobody here in the past because the past does not exist.
There will be nobody in the future because it never arrives.
The world is over because it never began.
Nothing has ever happened.

—